FRITZ KREISLER
FAVORITE ENCORES

To access audio visit:
www.halleonard.com/mylibrary

3520-8937-9071-0944

ISBN 978-1-59615-194-9

EXCLUSIVELY DISTRIBUTED BY

7777 W. BLUEMOUND RD. P.O. BOX 13819 MILWAUKEE, WI 53213

Visit Hal Leonard Online at
www.halleonard.com

DANIELA SHTEREVA

Daniela Shtereva, presently studying at the state Academy of Music in Sofia, Bulgaria, has performed as soloist with the Shumen Philharmonic, the Kardjali Chamber Orchestra, the Pazardjik Symphony Orchestra of Bulgaria, and has toured in Germany and Belgium as well as performing and recording for Bulgarian Radio and TV.

Daniela has also appeared as soloist and recorded with the Plovdiv Philharmonic Orchestra. She has consistently placed in the top ranks of competitions in Europe, taking first prize in the First Bulgarian Academic Competition in 1994, and second prize in the Fifth International Competition for Violinists in Fermo, Italy in 1998.

Her repertoire in classical music encompasses the 18th, 19th, and 20th centuries and includes film music. We are pleased to offer this second publication in this series by Daniela Shtereva of repertoire performed by the noted and much beloved Fritz Kreisler during his career.

JOSEPH SEIGER

Joseph Seiger, born in Rishon-le-Zion, Israel, started his music studies at the age of six. World War II interrupted these studies and the beginning of his career. During WWII Mr. Seiger served with the U.S. Army in Africa and the Middle East. In 1951, he graduated from the Manhattan School of Music where he was the first winner of the Harold Bauer Memorial Prize given for outstanding pianistic achievement. In the fall of 1952, Mr. Seiger auditioned for the eminent violinist Mischa Elman and was chosen to be his exclusive accompanist.

During the decades of the '50s and '60s, Mr. Seiger appeared with Mr. Elman in concert tours throughout the United States, Canada, South America, South Africa, Europe, Australia, New Zealand, and Japan. He also recorded some of the major works of the violin repertoire with Mr. Elman for RCA Victor, London, and Vanguard.

Mr. Seiger has appeared as a soloist in recitals and with orchestras both here and abroad.

Music Minus One

3165

Fritz Kreisler Favorite Encores

Allegretto - *Fritz Kreisler*   4

Ballet Music from *Rosamunde* - *Schubert/Kreisler*   6

La Precieuse in style of Couperin - *Fritz Kreisler*   8

Larghetto - *Weber/Kreisler*   10

Mazurka in A minor, Op. 67, No. 4 - *Chopin/Kreisler*   12

Polichinelle (Serenade) - *Fritz Kreisler*.   14

Serenade Espagnole - *Glazunov/Kreisler*   16

Shepherd's Madrigal - *Fritz Kreisler*   18

Song Without Words - *Mendelssohn/Kreisler*   21

Tambourin - *Fritz Kreisler*   22

Allegretto
(in the style of Niccolo Porpora)

Fritz Kreisler

5 taps (1 2/3 measures)
precede music.

Allegretto con ritmo

3165

3165

Ballet Music from

Rosamunde

Schubert - Kreisler

Allegretto moderato

La Precieuse

(in the style of Couperin)

7 taps (3 ½ measures)
precede music.

Fritz Kreisler

Allegretto con spirito

9

Larghetto

Weber-Kreisler

5 taps (2 ½ Measures)
precede music

Andante con moto.

con espressione ma molto semplice

Mazurka

in A minor

(Posthumous)Op.67,No.4

Chopin - Kreisler

5 taps (1 2/3 measures)
precede music.

Moderato animato

poco rit. a tempo

cresc. e poco accel. a tempo

cresc.

f p con calore

IIIª rubato con sentimento

cresc.

delicatissimo

p poco rit.

IIª Iª semplice

Violin

⊓ = Down bow
V = Up bow
T = Tip of the bow
N = Nut of the bow
M = Middle of the bow

Polichinelle
Serenade

Fritz Kreisler

Allegro giocoso e ritmico

più tranquillo

3165

poco a poco accel.

3165

SÉRÉNADE ESPAGNOLE

Alexander Glazunov, Op.20 No.2

*Transcribed for Violin and Piano
by Fritz Kreisler*

3165

Shepherd's Madrigal

FRITZ KREISLER

Poco meno mosso
rustico e ritmico

molto staccato

sempre cresc.

3165

poco a poco dim.

poco a poco rit.

Tempo I

cresc.

III   II   grazioso

III V

poco rit.

a tempo   *pp perdendosi e riten.*

Song Without Words

May Breeze, op.62, No.1

MENDELSSOHN-KREISLER

3165

Tambourin
(in the style of Leclair)

FRITZ KREISLER

Allegro con spirito e leggiero